1990

The Black Riviera

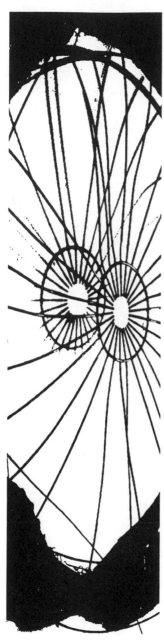

The Black Riviera

Mark Jarman

Wesleyan University Press
Middletown, Connecticut

New Narrative
New Formalism

Copyright © 1990 by Mark Jarman

The Poet's Prize 1991

Acknowledgment is made to the following magazines, in which some of these poems first appeared, some in a different version: *Crazyhorse, The Hudson Review, The Missouri Review, The New Yorker* ("The Black Riviera"), *The Ohio Review, Partisan Review, Pequod, Ploughshares, Poetry* ("Days of '74"), and *Poetry Northwest*. "Sea-Fig" is reprinted from *Prairie Schooner*, by permission of University of Nebraska Press, copyright © 1989 by University of Nebraska Press. "The Gift" first appeared in *The Music of What Happens: Poems That Tell Stories*, Orchard Books, 1988, copyright © 1988 by Orchard Books.

"Between Flights" was awarded a Pushcart Prize and appeared in *Pushcart XIII*.

The author wishes to thank the National Endowment for the Arts for a grant that aided in the completion of this book.

Library of Congress Cataloging-in-Publication Data

Jarman, Mark.
    The black Riviera.

    (Wesleyan poetry)
    I. Title. II. Series.
PS3560.A537B5   1989   811'.54   88-28075
ISBN 0-8195-2170-1
ISBN 0-8195-1172-2 (pbk.)

Manufactured in the United States of America

FIRST EDITION

WESLEYAN POETRY

First printing, 1990

b. 1952 Kentucky

Lit influences:
Edwin Arlington Robinson
Robert Frost
Robinson Jeffers

J's grandfather began preaching as a teenager

sim. agendas

~ The New
England
Rev.
The Hudson
Rev

J. met @ UCSC

For Robert McDowell

⌐ w/ Jarman co. founded
& edited The Reaper journal
(→1989)
also Story Line Press
(now imprint of Red Hen)

Issue 4: "The poet must comprehend that his
story is more important than his feelings
about it."

Contents

The Black Riviera

The Children

The children are hiding among the raspberry canes.
They look big to one another, the garden small.
Already in their mouths this soft fruit
That lasts so briefly in the supermarket
Tastes like the past. The gritty wall,
Behind the veil of leaves, is hollow.
There are yellow wasps inside it. The children know.
They know the wall is hard, although it hums.
They know a lot and will not forget it soon.

When did we forget? But we were never
Children, never found where they were hiding
And hid with them, never followed
The wasp down into its nest
With a fingertip that still tingles.
We lie in bed at night, thinking about
The future, always the future, always forgetting
That it will be the past, hard and hollow,
Veiled and humming, soon enough.

The Black Riviera

For Garrett Hongo

There they are again. It's after dark.
The rain begins its sober comedy,
Slicking down their hair as they wait
Under a pepper tree or eucalyptus,
Larry Dietz, Luis Gonzalez, the Fitzgerald brothers,
And Jarman, hidden from the cop car
Sleeking innocently past. Stoned,
They giggle a little, with money ready
To pay for more, waiting in the rain.

They buy from the black Riviera
That silently appears, as if risen,
The apotheosis of wet asphalt
And smeary-silvery glare
And plush inner untouchability.
A hand takes money and withdraws,
Another extends a sack of plastic—
Short, too dramatic to be questioned.
What they buy is light rolled in a wave.

They send the money off in a long car
A god himself could steal a girl in,
Clothing its metal sheen in the spectrum
Of bars and discos and restaurants.
And they are left, dripping rain
Under their melancholy tree, and see time
Knocked akilter, sort of funny,
But slowing down strangely, too.
So, what do they dream?

They might dream that they are in love
And wake to find they are,
That outside their own pumping arteries,
Which they can cargo with happiness
As they sink in their little bathyspheres,
Somebody else's body pressures theirs
With kisses, like bursts of bloody oxygen,
Until, stunned, they're dragged up,
Drawn from drowning, saved.

In fact, some of us woke up that way.
It has to do with how desire takes shape.
Tapered, encapsulated, engineered
To navigate an illusion of deep water,
Its beauty has the dark roots
Of a girl skipping down a high-school corridor
Selling Seconal from a bag,
Or a black car gliding close to the roadtop,
So insular, so quiet, it enters the earth.

Human Geography

Sometimes I feel the whole coast in my body.
At night, homesick, this helps me get to sleep.
Sand lies along my arm. Along the sand lies
The outer pressure of all otherness,
The twinning, twining ocean, gray or blue
As the sky, black or green as depths and shallows.
The rows of houses salted by its break,
The roads peppered with sand, the thick shells crushed
By riptides, tangle like limbs and weeds and water.
But honestly, this wholeness is a segment.
At most a draft sets off a memory.
Skin prickling, eye flickering, a taste of brine,
And I detect the heat of a summer sidewalk
That dips and rises with the coastal hills
Where wild oat, chaparral, and live oak now
Are stucco houses scraping the fog's body,
That vapor that burns to vapor by afternoon.
The heat comes up, the hills descend and rise.
A friend grimaces as a bit of glass
Pierces his heel, grinding toward the bone.
He sits down on a lawn, just like a tailor,
Pinching the heel. It pouts a bead of blood.
And I go up to someone's door for a needle.
She stares at me out of a massive brightness,
On such a hot day, blazing inside her house,
Where glaring lamps and reflectors lean toward
Something stretched out behind her. The borrowed needle
Feels itself like a burning line of glass.
And when I turn away, the day seems dark,
Darker as her door clicks. She calls, "Keep it!"
About the needle. Out, the spike of glass
Is now invisible. The sequence, too—
My age, my friend's identity, the woman—
Invisible. Here's when the stucco town
Grates like a shell to powder vague as fog
And turns so smooth, the flanges, hinges, spurs,
The spicules and ridges sanded off,
Hushing itself to sleep without a name,

Softening, sieving fact and leaving fiction.
And that is when I nearly fall asleep.
But this can happen anytime. Awake,
I drive all roads at once, wired with passion.
It's always a surprise. I can never think,
"Now I will feel the town where I grew up
And brand it to myself here, far away."
A gift—the feeling that flesh itself is a place
And not, banal reliance, just the body,
Working as always—but another thing.
Then, I can drive back into a story,
Any I choose, and pick it out again.
My friend, heel in his hands, picks at the wound,
A short, compact, fierce boy, fighting his pain.
I am afraid to bother anyone.
But he demands I go to the front door
And beg a needle. No, it needs no fire.
The glass is just below the heel's callus.
We're 12 years old this summer. At the beach,
The offshore winds of afternoon have raised
Those rare, scooped-out, fast-running, light
Breakers for body surfing that we like.
I go to the door, knock, and it's jerked open.
The body in it's just a silhouette
Of shade and heat, a sunspot on the sun.
Then black distinctions, crisp, cut-out, appear,
Her curls of hair, the knots of bathing suit,
Then cloth lines, pale flesh crescents, thigh and breast.
She answers with a question, cutting quickly,
And disappears. And I can't help but see it,
Stretched out like a bed or body, what the lamps
And the reflectors and the camera point at:
A city done in miniature, a model,
No one, nothing, else. The needle in my palm,
She says, "I'm a photographer."
                              And so,
I tell my friend, as he forgets the pain
Long past the house and nearly to the beach,

That in that house, hidden under the lights,
I've seen what neither of us has ever seen,
Even where flesh is sand, down at the beach,
Exposed and everywhere, and yet and yet—
I saw her and the camera set to take her.
And so the story grows, as he colludes
With me, encircled by our friends. It adds
Whole tracts and housing projects, as her body
Grows vast, its clarity as painful as
The needle in the heel, which she herself,
As we recount it, worked with surgeon's care.
Friends beg to know the address—just the block!—
But know those stucco houses shunting down
The low hills to the sea. Parched, salty lawns.
Those pastel boxes turning one shell-white.
Besides, we've both been sworn to secrecy.
The story, relaxed, elaborate, runs on.
Now she is dressed, now only in bathing suit.
She is a man, or man and woman. There is
A bed of nails, then just a bed. We both
Were brought inside, then only one. We fled.
We stayed. The story tumbles on through tides,
Cadenzas, raveling, unraveling.
Awake, I can recall what happened to it.
Awake, the Pacific urges me to sleep.
And I must squeeze the wheel, if I am driving,
Or wince with pain, as if I have been lying
On a beach of broken shells.

Awakened by Sea Lions

They crowd their rookery, the dilapidated outcrop
The ocean gives a bubble-top of glass to at high tide.
Among them two or three of the four-ton elephant seals
Loll pathetically, like queen bees without hives.
The lions call out. Insomniac, late, the fog a loose curtain
Of moonshot aquatic light, restless and static,
    They speak.

But not to us. Nor to the ocean. I have heard
One daughter wake on her top bunk sobbing
And her younger sister below ask her what's wrong.
Deep in the night, all of us waking to her cry.
"What's wrong?" And then, "I can't sleep."
Just the two of them. Silence again. Slumber.
    The call comes

Out of the vast peaceful mere rimmed by new worlds.
And those who hear it are soothed, even though
It might rise from throats that gulp pale fish
Torn out of the wave, from inelegant chimeras
    With limbs like dolphins',
Dog-eared, whiskered like cats, mouths set
With human teeth. The call travels its distance.
Once heard, it travels further.

The Mystic

For Chris Buckley

It just doesn't occur to you where there are only skinny
    palms
And sunburn-pink houses and wide avenues and the
    aluminum plane
Of the Pacific that anything is secret. Where are the vaulted
    elms, the brick
Aged like wine, the dreary weather to plaster elm leaves on
    aged brick?
Yet, I knew a mystic there. He worked out of the sun, his
    one black suit
Showing a stitch of dandruff white as his face, and turned
    his gaze
Obliquely to words as true as he could say them. He
    worked—
But it didn't matter. Standing in the lobby of his movie
    house, beside the little harbor,
He lived, as he would say, outside the flesh. Up in his office
At the top of the double staircase, he crept through texts,
    gathering
Evidence like a seine net, odd fish mixed with phosphor.
He believed there were men whose offered palms
    produced, at a shrug,
Bread or even gold. That all light in the universe, all that
    we see,
Begins in the self. There is no outer light. And, believing, he
    lived another life.

Believe it, he said, there is more. What is extraordinary
    knowledge
But fingers adhering to a talisman essential as their own
    charm
Or what a gaze fixes on in a corner of the ceiling?
Take the TV set he owned, its gray-green bulging face that,
When the picture filled it like a speechless, readable
    expression,
Dangled a sooty web over the heads of the colorless actors.
You saw it, it was part of the picture, just over their heads,
    calligraphy
Of another world encroaching and sending its messages.

After World War II, he said he walked past houses
    wondering how
The people in them woke and went to bed and in between
    went on with life.
That was the beginning. Now he knew the hidden was like
    a parent, thinking
She must this second turn off the light in her child's room,
Late, the TV telling its sick jokes, and when she entered,
    finding
The two-year-old ill on her pillow. The occult greets its
    initiates.

That's how I think of him in this world, where the engine
    block
Cracks on the snowy interstate, and the life it held—
    searing,
True—escapes with a hiss. He stands to the side, letting me
Ask him questions as the light brooms in, straw gold, tinged
With all it's touched in the harbor, the tourist boats and
    chum tanks
And the breakwater's combs of seaweed. We stand in the
    movie-house lobby,
Anteroom to the dark, the muttering auditorium where, on
    a sun-stroked afternoon,
Only a few sit, harmless. I ask about Jacob's ladder, the
    language dolphins exchange.
He knows. And, here is the secret, he knows it is a secret
    pursuit, the questioning and answering.
Under the chains biting the ice and the tow truck
    delivering the day
And the bill, there is another road. A former day fumes
Outside, and inside its light lies at our feet. The ocean
    seeps
Under the building, and the pier rats throw their shadows
    against the screen,
And one patron, furious from the darkness, won't believe
    our disbelief.

The Shrine and the Burning Wheel

On the way to the evening reading,
Stopped at a Quick Stop for cigarettes,
I saw, as did everyone else parked there
Or passing, a gang of boys,
    Local boys probably,
Burning the front wheel of a ten-speed.
The bicycle, turned upside down,
Stood on the dumpster side of the store,
And one boy glanced from the corner
    Through the front window.
    Transcendence, that's what
It means to want to be gone
As, turning the eye's corner
To the sudden glare of fire,
The local terror stares in your face.
    I got the hell out of there,
And kept the spidery intaglio
Of the one, their lookout, peeping
Into the store window at—it must have been—
    The boy who owned the bicycle
    In his clerk smock
    Making change from the safe.
At the evening reading, as the poet was
Introduced at length, she rested her head
    On the heel of her left hand,
    Full hair falling to the propped elbow,
And, as the prologue ran on,
Shook a little dandruff from her hair.
And what I saw was no longer her gesture
But the memory of Nora and Bo Dee Foster
    And the crowd at the Shrine Auditorium
    In Los Angeles, long ago, listening
To "Renascence" and "A Few Figs from Thistles"
And one that rhymed "stripèd pants" and "Paris, France."
    Bo Dee remembers how
    As Huxley went on
And on introducing her,
Edna Millay shook the dandruff from her hair.

Transcendence is not
Going back
To feel the texture of the past
Like the velvet nap of the loges
In the Shrine. It is wanting to be
   Anywhere else.
   Clearly, I don't understand.
The wheel spins. It is not hard to ignite
The hard lean tire with lighter fluid.
It flashes and a round of smiles
Breaks in the dismal circle
   Of the boy pack
   From the apartment complexes.
In their stripèd pants they open doors
Of sedans to men in maroon fezzes.
But they are men themselves, Nobles,
And wear ruby rings set with diamonds
   And symbols.
Searchlights mortar the clear night.
"Thank you, Noble," says one man
Helping his wife to the curb.
   She, white as a fez's tassel,
   And the grandchildren
Will see a Chinese girl prodigy at the piano,
Jugglers on unicycles,
And, the reason they've come,
   Edgar Bergen and Charlie McCarthy,
   Aging and never to age.
Here at the Shrine, with its swag tent ceiling
And Arabic signs, hands of the crowd
   Grip in ways
   That cannot be revealed.
   But now the amps are on.
Big Brother and the Holding Company are on.
The rapid fire of strobes cuts, cuts.
But that's too much, too soon.
   Instead, it's the Boy Scout Expo.
   Let it be calm for a while

As it would be at a state fair
Inside a great pavilion.
    Here are the Scouts displaying
    Their skill at fly casting.
    The arc ends in a splash.
Fly-blue or fly-green, it hits the pool
Among the crowd, under the roof
Of the Shrine Hall. There is quiet.
Then a cheer. Now the speakers start up.
    Janis Joplin, shapeless and small
In the loose madras fabric of her dress,
Flares and thrashes in the wind
    Her body makes to the music,
    Cut and cut and cut
    By the strobe lights across her hair.
Transcendence is what she wants
Or not what she wants, to live
In the world or out of it,
    To be anywhere else
    Or here, as a studied voice
Says its poetry of heaven and earth,
And meshed with it, hidden,
A wheel of history turns,
And the boys burn the wheel.

Between Flights

You won't need to make a story up about us.
If you have overheard us, then you know
The one we're telling each other will do.
It's about an everyday catastrophe
That makes us wonder if our childhood
Was all we thought it was, a place
We have left but that remains intact.
I have a layover and my sister has brought
Her baby with her to chat for my two hours.
She drove out through the flat tangled miles
Of lunchtime traffic. Luckily, the baby
Is happy and sang to her, screeching his joy
And throwing his body in its fits of pleasure
Against the car-seat straps. He's freer now
To lunge out of his high chair at our coffee.
We can't change our lives to bring them closer.
The plate-glass window by our table
Turns a kind of photographic gray
When the clouds baffle the sun, then blue again.
I can't keep from noticing, below us,
The space outdoors filled with patterned traffic
Coming and going in the terminal
Over and under causeways, and, above us, the sky,
What's visible, with the same geometry.
She's worried that her baby's eczema
Will stay with him for life, but already,
Using a different diet and way of washing him,
She's erased the itchy-looking scales
Around his neck—there's just a ring of dryness
Circling his mouth. Joy works him like
A spring, popping him up, and people's heads turn.
That's how we've gotten attention. But our talk
Is only an old story, one you know.
We live so far apart, we're now the ages
Our parents were, etc. Except, last year,
It ended—their life together stopped.
The worst part is now we talk about them
As if they both were dead and not going on

Separately. Our conversation stops
The moment the baby sweeps my plate
To the floor. But that makes us smile
Ruefully, pick up the pieces, try
To calm him with a muffin he can gnaw on
And let him scatter crumbs instead.
Consider this, listeners around us.
We protect within ourselves the secrecy
That is the code to our happiness, the black box
Recorded with the last message of childhood.
My sister and I could play it back for you
But it would make no sense. I even wonder
If it would sound like gibberish to us.
Doesn't it describe another country,
And in that country a coastal town,
And in that town, set in a gray row
With others like it, an oblong garden
Where summer hangs like a pane of glass
Slanting toward its fall? A hailstone
Or meteor, so high it seems to drift,
Aims at it, then rushes suddenly, and
Suddenly, it's gone. A tiny missile,
No bigger than a key that scalds the hand,
Shatters summer, garden, childhood.
How commonplace, that we cannot explain
Ourselves, that all we can give you is
Our brisk completion now it's time to leave,
Our kisses, our regards, and our good-byes.

Days of '74

What was the future then but affirmation,
The first *yes* between us
Followed by the first lingering dawn?
Waking below a window shaded by redwoods
(Waking? We hadn't slept—),
We found time saved, like sunlight in a tree.

Still, the house was cold, and there were shadows.
The couple in the next room
Rapped the wall to quiet us, like them,
Condescending from a bitter knowledge
That, young as we all were,
Love didn't last, but receded into silence.

Wedging our pillows back of the headboard
That clapped in time with us,
We let them think we agreed. Then, holding on,
We closed each other's mouths and felt that slowness
That the best days begin with
Turn into the speed with which they fly.

Flight was that year's theme, all around us—
Flight of hunter and hunted,
The President turning inward on one wing,
And, on the patio, the emigration
Of termites, a glittering fleet,
Leaving that shadowed house a little lighter.

Within it all, above it, or beyond,
We thought we were the fixed point,
And held still as the quail lit down beside us
And waited for her plump mate to appear,
His crest a quivering hook.
The valley's reach of sunshine reeled them in.

There was wilderness around us, don't forget.
Behind the nets of fragrance
Thrown across our path by the acacia
Lurked the green man or the kidnapper.
And there was the Pacific
With its own passions taking place as rain.

The sorrow of the couple in the next room
Was a deep muteness nightly.
That loneliness could come of loving was
Like news of time cored out of the redwood.
The house that we made shake,
Or thought we did, was taking wing already.

After we left, still it took us years
Before we stopped comparing
Every morning together to that first one
And every place we lived to that first place
And everything we said
To that first word repeated all night long.

Good Friday

Heat is what I imagine, dust and tension,
And by midafternoon the cloudburst,
The sudden coolness, a balm for some, none
For those who had seen a loved one die,
Horribly, nails through his wrists, suffocating,
If not bleeding to death, in the heat, the tension.
The rain covered the gap of his life,
A rattling screen of iridescent beads
Pummeling the dust, cutting off our view.

It does no good to forecast the weather
Backwards. If it was tempest weather,
The nails bit the wood thirsting for sap,
The grain split with a hoarse cough.
Then rain fell. The woods filled with freshness,
Sandal thongs gleamed, faces basked.
Verisimilitude is magic. Jesus struggled
For breath, hanging forward, and said little.
Then someone prodded him, but he was dead.

He lived. He died. He knew what was happening.
The night my father came home from Claremont
And sat at the foot of my bed, forcing up
The news of D.'s death, was a Good Friday.
D.'s bowels had locked and starved his brain
Of blood. He died screaming, and in silence.
There were no last coherent words,
And his young wife (both of them so young)
Had curled between his deathbed and the wall.

All this my father told me.
And the story of D.'s life was told,
Friend by friend, a dozen lives.
A year later there was a gathering
To view home movies of him, and a film
He'd made, mostly a lyric reel
Of widening water circles—
Loved because his eye had seen them,
Turned the lens to ingest the light.

D. died when I was 16. I remember
His twenty-fourth birthday, his last,
The strobe lights' percussion, Zorba music,
And him dancing because that was the soul:
Rhythmless, bare-chested, leaping in air,
Really, I think, in all the sweat and shouting,
To prove a man could dance that way,
In a church basement, a man could
With another man, their wives clapping.

They say that Jesus died at 33.
They say so, and now I think I believe it.
Never have my age and others' ages
Seemed so real, so physically what they are.
I see the skin's grain, the back's curve,
The pools of stamina drawn carefully
To contain the world no longer vast
In possibilities, except that it
Can kill, even in your prime.

And yet, 30, a craftsman in wood,
One finally thought he knew what humankind
Wanted—to be loved, to be forgiven,
Which meant to be loved always.   26
And yes, perhaps, he was a little naive.
He believed that this was possible,
Loved as he had been by his mother,
His father who trained him to work wood.
He knew the feel of love's grain, its texture.

Knew a way, too, to speak of love.
It had a substance, a heft, like wood
Or nets or sacks of seed or jars of ointment.
Things came to mind, they came to hand,
Unscrolling even from the written word.
The world was made of love, to love.
And he was on the road, finding listeners.
And he was of an age when he knew doom
Waited for him, that people heard what they wanted.

That is, they heard what they lacked.
The glory of it turned the desert green.
The cedars' vertical aspiration said it.
Roads offered their dust, their thieves.
Cities congregated suspiciously, busy
And explosive with potential. Teacher,
They called him (as they called others):
Everyone must be included, loved,
The excluded most of all, who would doom him.

They say he taught three years. They say
Much about him, that his life
Was seamless, like his robe.
And, yet, he was that age when,
Seamed, you put away childish things
And take children into your arms.
They would doom him. He entered rooms
Forbidden to be entered, where the dead
Lay, rising at his call, to doom him.

None of it worked him well. But look,
He lived into his prime,
With all those years to go before
The oil of mother's cooking, the shavings
Of occupational hazard, would paralyze him.
Therefore, the risk of loving this way
Dripped, a water clock; flared, a lamp
Sucking up fuel. It became his disease,
Willed and unwilled, breath held and released.

Heat is what I imagine, dust and tension.
The scourging I imagine he understood,
The soldiers' reviling, surely he had seen that,
And the way crucifixion worked, the need to
Break legs to bring the strangulation on
(No need in his case; he'd already gone).
In the cloudburst, the downpour of signs,
The saints out walking, puzzled to be raised,
Things were torn, shattered, terrifying.

Today, the lawns are clouded with at least
Six kinds of wild flower. Ground ivy,
Corn speedwell, henbit, chickweed,
Spring beauties, and the dandelion.
My daughters know their names. My wife
And I look at them, the girls and flowers,
And none of us thinks of him, who does not
Haunt us, any more than anyone gone,
When there is such a theodicy of blossoms.

Our four-year-old's lips nearly touch
A dandelion globe, spluttering,
As she learns to blow the seeds away.
One night, the sepals close on golden petals,
Then open, changed. Gone to seed.
Gone to worlds of possibility.
What's love, even eternal love,
But evolution to endure? And doesn't it
Begin here, learning to blow a kiss?

Yes, it is complex, I know.
Look at the articulation of the seed itself,
The filament erect to its parachute
Of downy hairs. How easily
It could be taken as almost cruciform,
How willingly the wind could explicate it:
His breath, his sign. But it is ours,
As we show her how to force the air
Out in a rush, our love she takes as her own.

Story Hour

What were they saying, the storytellers,
The newsbringers, the parablists,
The fabulists, the gathered tribe
Of the living room, the forgetful ones?
Even in the stories they told,
If the pieces that came clear fitted right,
They did not remember this desperation
To know, that sent a tense child off
To a tense sleep, dropping him, helpless noun,
Through the smoky verbs of his own body,
Throwing out images even more meaningless
    Than a few sweet words
Fitted together to predict a calm future,
The one that, for all their demurrals,
The grown ones had reached and told of
    In these stories at night.

The talk lived in the panel of wall
Between my bedroom and the living room,
The chalky membrane of plaster
    Deaf to the higher insinuations
And passing along chronicles and apologues
Of lower voices, full of lacunae,
Fragments in a burning hand written
On less than water—air—
Across the oval blank of my vision
    And funneling down the ear.

No trees outside except the distant eucalyptus.
Only the surf's voice at night.
Trees need wind, but on the stillest night
The waves spoke like leaves.
And, like a spasm of phosphor,
    Through the wall an adult confided
And another caught the glimmer,
Gave it heart and luster simply

By a laugh or beckoning denial or sighing
Affirmation. Outside the house
On its hill of clay and sand and dry grass,
    No trees. The waves were the leaves.

We lived in a lath-and-plaster house,
Mud and sticks, pimpled with stucco,
On a sand hill above the Pacific,
Two slabs of concrete and a wood floor, a trilevel,
    My bedroom on the lowest.
I knew where the termite built its palaces,
The king snake and the snail
Sheltered under ice plant and ivy,
The velvet ant took the sun
On its blazing hair, and the black widow
    Hoarded her power.
And I listened, when I went to bed,
To the strange language of adults
    At story hour.

What *were* they saying, as they built
A wing on the night, closed off
As the carpentry echoed back beyond the work wall,
    And the glaring work lights
Could only be guessed at, by the confidence
Of the faint voices? There was no groping
For words among them. It was the listener
    Who groped, bound to bed
By drowsiness, breath balled up like a rag
To stop the loud heart.

The head, the room, the house, the world,
The journey out is a passing through doors
After the eyes open, if they open.
    The stasis of sleep prevents this
And propels it spirally through dream,
Past the drowning urge

To keep the open book from falling face down.
The head, the room, the house
Begin where the human is a voice
And the voice a story and the story
        An episode and the episode
A sandman's powder of mumbling and sighs.

The room, the house, the world
Can only be traveled this way. *Get up.*
Walk out the door, down the hall,
Up the stairs and into the living room
        Where they still chatter. Their voices
Begin to sharpen like stones when a pool stills.
Only, the pool is your listening, the house's tumult.
Still it by entering. First, they will frown,
        Falling silent,
And their final smiles will nail the night shut.

        They always knew
        What their child wanted to hear
And never quite caught, slipping
Through the hazy light of their voices.
There was a real prize.
        Should they tell him?
"Those nights you lay awake
And we, having waited until you went to bed,
Began to share our news
        Or listened to a friend or stranger
Lay out a plot before us
Like a simple or intricate gift
Unwrapped on a coffee table
        Or extended across the living-room floor—

Yes, you were missing something.
And what if an occasional clue,
A mere gnat of an episode, flitted
Into your hearing. So young then,
    You could only have built
    A dream or nightmare out of it.

"It is too late to tell you
Any of what you missed, largely
Because we have forgotten, and possibly,
Now you are grown, because you have heard it all
    And repeated to yourself, wisely,
'This old story of his or hers—
I know it already.' And sometimes
You have said so to us, cruelly,
And pushed it, this tale of our identities,
    Away like a hug or a kiss."

Now I want to dream, but the velvet ant
Exits from a sugary ridge of sand,
A downy automaton, and the king snake,
Colder than the spikes of ice plant,
Makes a black track, snails smash,
Hurled against the garden wall,
A line of lighter fluid traces
Termites into their halls,
Fire follows. I want to dream
    All is forgiven and these bones—
The speaking of water
And the distance of eucalyptus—
Will make a past, parents, a child.
But I cannot dream beyond
    The creatures of the sand hill,
Velvet ant, king snake, snail, termite,
And in every hollow the black widow's
    Speckled daughters.

I believe there is a secret to life
Because my earliest memories are
Of hearing secrets muffled by a wall,
Coming to me in pieces like dust
Sliding down a shaft of sunlight.
    Only these came in darkness
And sparked and fused and radiated
Half-truths I made whole.

It is story hour on the hilltop.
The blue sea looks up at the sky.
The foxtails point with the breeze,
    The sinless, culprit breeze.
And everyone's gone, except
As this dream I wanted to dream.

"You wanted to hear us assure you
That there was only one story,
And that story a promise
    Of never-ending love,
    That you would love us
Just as a child loves his parents
And we would love you
In the same, unchanging way
And each other, telling the same stories,
Long after you had grown and gone,
    To no one listening
    In his deserted room.
The one story that is never told
But thought of as if it had been,
As a perfect story, none better,
    Is of a love nobody keeps."

15

Dreaming, I say to my mother and father,
"By the power vested in me
I pronounce you lost, irrevocably."
They laugh. I have no such power.
They are turned into eucalyptus trees
Rained on by the same weather
    On different continents.

The Gift

When I was five my father kidnapped me. 18
He didn't keep me long enough to worry
My mother. And I wonder if she knew.
But I knew, five years old. That day at school,
He waited for me at the double doors,
His Hudson parked behind him, ready to go.
I knew he'd come when he was not supposed to.
He said it was all right, my mother knew.
On the front seat, there was a present for me,
And as he started, he said I could unwrap it.
The ribbon wouldn't give, the gift box buckled.
But he was driving, couldn't stop to help.
Outside the windshield traffic lights hung down
From cables, and the bushy tops of palms
Showed up at intervals that I could count.
A pink or yellow building front skimmed past.
But mostly I could only see the sky.
A child could hardly see from those old cars
With the window set up high above your shoulder.
The sky went by, pale blue and white and empty,
Crossed suddenly by wire. And I gave up
Trying to take the wrapping off my present
Until we reached wherever we were going.
Then, at a stop, one of those tall palm trees
That wears a shaggy collar of dead fronds
Leaned down and opened up the door and got in
Beside me. Daddy called her Charlotte dear
And told her I was Susan. Sitting down,
She was the tallest woman, and she wore
A high fur collar with white points of hair.
She let me put my hand on them. So soft!
I was excited then, because she helped me
Unwrap my gift and set me on her lap
So I could see. It was a long drive then,
Through orange groves where all the fruit was green,
Past dairy farms that you could smell right through
The rolled-up windows and even through the sweetness

29

Of Charlotte's perfume and Daddy's after-shave.
We went down through a canyon to the beach
And Charlotte pointed at a pair of wings,
Two bars of black and white that drifted high
Above the gap. She said it was a condor.
Against the ocean, where the canyon ended,
A roller coaster's highest hump rose up.
Beside it was a dome with colored flags.
By this time in the afternoon, at home,
Mother would listen to the radio
And pretty soon I'd have to go indoors
For dinner. Daddy bought me a corn dog,
An Orange Julius, and, for dessert,
The biggest cotton candy in the world.
But first I rode the carousel three times.
From there, as I pumped slowly up and down,
I had a good look at the two of them—
Daddy, like a blond boulder, round and bald,
And Charlotte, though I knew how soft she was,
Like a palm tree still, looking stiff and spiky.
I knew he loved me (maybe she did, too),
But soon he'd have to take me home to Mother.
Around us broke a bank of evening fog,
Softly but coldly, too. We had to leave.
Later I fell asleep on Charlotte's arm,
Her fox fur floating lightly on my hair
And Daddy's present open on my lap.
I wish I'd kept awake to have my say
That day, that one day clearer than all my childhood.
Next morning I awoke in my own bed,
And Mother asked if I'd had fun with Daddy.
He'd kidnapped me. She didn't seem to know it!
Daddy and Charlotte never married. Mother
Went on as if he were a kindly neighbor
Dropping in now and then to help her with me.
We'll see if that's the way I treat your father.
I can't recall what the gift was he gave me.

Liechtenstein

For Audrey Rugg

Two white whales, the father and the bolster
He hugs to his sour guts. Something he ate.
High up in the hotel room the roof beams,
Carved with bluebirds and red crocuses,
Are thatched with shadows. Hammocks
Of cobweb luff in the rising heat. His wife
Is leafing through a guide. His children finger
New purchases, the girl her dirndl skirt,
The boy his Swiss watch with its 17 jewels,
Already a glinting scratch across the crystal.
August, a rainy month in this small country.
Window-framed, the castle's topped with mist.
Now he is snoring, whom the doctor sighed for
Listening to his chronicle that accused
Last night's Italian dinner: "Ah, but you're
A foreigner." At last now, he's asleep,
The bolster, a man-long pillow, in his arms.

Out in the little capital, the day
Above the mother and her boy and girl
Combs out a cloud of rain that hangs and drifts
And lapses over the castle's roofs and windows.
The children ask her questions about the prince
And reason that, because he's just a prince
And his castle small, he might accept a visit.
But Mother says the way looks wet and steep.
They find a *Konditorei* of covered tables,
Sober as snow in a deserted square,
Where statuelike two pairs of men are seated
At separate tables. All four eat ice cream.
Two of them whisper head to head. The others,
An old man and his younger version, smile.
The mother lets her children say the French
For ice cream, and at once the old man speaks.
His elephant ears are nests of silver hair,
His bald head faintly blue with broken vessels.
He compliments the girl's black braids, the boy's
White-blondness and their mother's youth and beauty,
Nimble with English and with flattery.

The pale ice cream tastes sweeter than its color,
Like the flesh of pears and apples, and comes heaped
In glasses shaped like tulips that, when empty,
Reveal a smoky tinge and weigh no more,
It seems, than ash or cobwebs. "A pretty place,
Our country," says the old man. And they nod,
Despite the weather. He admires the watch,
The dirndl skirt now spotted with ice cream,
And frowns to learn that Father, at the hotel,
Is sick and sleeping. "It is a pretty place,"
He says again, as rain begins, clear strands
That catch the window, then the falling rush.
"You would not think it an unhappy place.
Yet, like America, it has a past,
An older past, of course, and just as sad.
Our little country gave up one in ten,
Three hundred years ago, three hundred out of
Three thousand—one in ten. But you, too, know
Of hunting witches in America.
Yet a *Kleinstaat* is like a little town.
Its jealousies let loose the wild assumption
Salvation could be won for the accused
And for the living peace of mind—with fire."

The woman and her children stare, enclosed
Now by the rain and this familiar voice.
"I know a tale of witches for your children."
The boy and girl swallow their ice cream slowly
And feel it down their throats, a cold paste.
The old man's young companion moves to speak,
But the woman looks intrigued. She leans and arches
Her fine American neck to hear. He sees it—
Sap gold as barkless fruitwood—and relaxes.
"The *Minnesängers* have an old love song.
My voice has hit its tree line or I'd sing it.
It goes that, hunting once for capercaillie
(You know them? Game birds, gallinaceous),
A hunter pierced a woman in a clearing.
When he bent down to her, to break the arrow,

He held a mass of feathers that squirted away.
He followed blood, like scarlet stitchery,
To a black hollow, slimy with dead leaves
Under a willow's root. There, he thrust in
His hand and found a passage he could walk down
Lit by a door ajar at the far end.
Through the door's crack he watched the witch, as you
Might watch one of your children dress for bed
When they are very young. He watched, but she
Was not a child and not a hag. The wound
Was near the heart. She wound the bandage—so."
And for the children, watching witnesses,
White O's of ice cream printed on their mouths,
He makes the winding motion, as if tying
The band around his chest. "She knew he watched.
Knew when the wound was dressed, he would be bound.
She made the knot. The door opened. She had him!
She gave him feathers, a capercaillie cock's,
And sent him out to do her autumn forage.
His plumage blurred among the evergreens.
His will was mute, his protests. Then, an arrow
Caught him on his first flight, and he was free.
This hunter was the daughter of a count.
She found him lying as he'd found the witch.
But he stayed human in her hands, oh yes,
And spoke to her, healed only by her touch,
Which was like polished fruitwood, smooth and cool.
She was amazed that, in a blinding second,
A bird lay in her arms a man. He spoke. . . ."

There is a flashbulb pop, without a light.
A second of dead breath. They turn to look
Beside them where the men were whispering,
The two men head to head with their ice cream.
And one of them looks back through his curled hands
And groans. The other holds the jagged stub
Of one of those glass tulips he has broken
In his friend's face. Now hubbub is translated
To tell the woman what the hurt man says.

"He says, 'What have you done?' " And the attacker,
Setting the broken glass down, shakes his head.
He says he does not know what he has done.
The children see the blood. Their mother sees,
And whisks them out the door. The rain has stopped.
At the hotel, the bolster against his thigh,
Like the pillar of salt Lot might have brought to bed,
Father's his old self, rolling out his greetings
Like timbers on a surge. He's ordered supper,
Been reading about Italy. What's wrong?
She tells him what she can, the men, the blood.
And the children tell him all about a story
Where birds are men and women hunt them, and
A bald man, witches burned here by the thousands.
Father feels weak again. The evening comes.

She meets the knock as if she knew and dreaded
That it would come, one hand against the door,
Pressing against it, the other on the knob,
A quiver from her running through the frame.
In bed, her husband, feeling better now,
Leans curiously. The children stand in bathrobes.
It is the storyteller's young companion,
The one who had translated the cries for her.
"I've come to make apologies, I hope.
That picture of our country was not true.
No truer than we get on television
Of your America. I came with gifts."
He gives each child a clear waxed envelope
That holds three postage stamps. "We make these things."
He draws his hand, the thumb and index pinched
Beside his temple, squinting. "We engrave them,
Uncle and I." The children peer at them,
Three rectangles of sun-struck reds and blues,
Embossed with charcoal tracery to make
Three windows of stained glass: a coat of arms,
A haloed woman holding a cathedral,
And one—they know her—Mary with her baby.
Small in the upper corners, there are landscapes

Made totally of sunlight. Bowing a little,
The children put the stamps back carefully,
Surprising Mother, and say, *"Merci. Danke."*
But when she turns to him as if to receive
A gift herself, he shows his empty hands.
"No, no." She smiles. "How did the story end?
The hunter was about to speak." "The story?
Ah, yes. First, let me say, it was not right
Even without an end. The enchanted bird
Makes many flights and comes back every time
With what he finds—grubs, grains—for the witch's winter.
He loves the witch, you see. His spell is love.
Shot by the countess, he is free. But still,
With the spell broken, he will have to die.
Another version has him just a bird
In love with a human being, doomed by his feelings.
They are big birds, these grouse. The horse of the woods."

Her husband nods and wakes, looking attentive,
A turtle poking out to catch the drift
He might have missed, doubting it was important.
She sees between them a fraternal sign—
Two men about to speak, turning away
From a woman and her children to that language
That, now she knows, can break glass in a face.
A splinter of this place, this little nowhere,
Glints as it works into her memory.
What has he suffered but an upset stomach?
What has he done but missed it all and made her
Witness to it alone, with children watching?
He nods inside his snowy mountain shell.
"You are ill, sir," the stamp engraver says.
"Yes. Something I ate last night. Cannelloni?"
"Possibly. But, of course, you are a stranger."

The Home

They went there one Sunday afternoon
With the manager of The Home,
Who wanted to show them how poor
Though decent the former facilities were,
And to take them to the construction site.
Some you will meet, he warned them,
Do not wish to move. And this
They understood, the three of them,
The committee representing The Committee.
And some do not know what is happening,
He confided, and some in fact
It will be difficult to move.
The broad pink stucco building
Bleached in the sunshine, and he nodded
Toward the upper story when he said "difficult."
The infirmary was there, under the roof.
Before the building, on the wide lawn
That spread like a shelf then sloped
Down to the loud highway,
A few residents in steel lawn chairs
Basked in the sunlight, distantly,
Small figures in ones, twos, threes.
The manager opened the entry door
And rattled it, which shook
Its squares of glass, and the committee
Shook their heads, too.
A small woman, neatly attired,
Met them and looked up in each face.
Her rosy scalp and sparse white hair
Looked fresh, and she shook everyone's hand.
Notice the linoleum floors,
Said the manager, they are laid on concrete.
And the nearly bald woman nodded.
She too would be glad to leave.
It's a Ford facility, she said,
But we try to give Cadillac care.
The committee murmured and smiled.
They looked along the arched ceiling
Where the fire sprinklers ran
And, heads tilted back, seemed to follow them

Behind the manager down the dim hall.
Doors were closed where residents
Were napping or, they could hear,
Watching their private TV's.
A band of harsh sunlight crossed ahead.
The solarium, said the manager.
There were bookshelves, one with glass doors.
A tall, angular man who said nothing
Passed them and lowered the blinds
On one window and sat with a book
In the brown dusk of a corner.
John, the manager said to him,
It's such a fine day outside.
John looked up from his book, put
A cigar in his mouth. Now, John,
The manager said, and touched the small woman's elbow.
She sat beside John and nodded good-bye.
The manager led the committee
Around the corner. The lower floor,
He said, is a U. This is the east wing,
And here, since he is out at the moment,
You can take a look at John's room.
It was a big room and looked out at a hedge
That grew too close for the window to open completely.
And look, the manager said, how stiff
These handles are, and cranked one.
Notice the heat register, too,
Steam heat, terribly dry.
Through chinks in the hedge they saw color.
Yes, that's the garden, he said.
And heard three flat, unrelated whistle notes.
The manager smiled. Our gardener.
Listen to this—he turned on the tap
At the sink—and the pipes banged and screeched.
But you know, John wants to stay.
There wasn't much to the room.
His bed near the window, a desk,
And the massive TV draped with lace

And covered on top with photographs.
The manager shut John's door softly.
Let's see the infirmary, he said.
Outside between wings they saw
A croquet game staked out
And, bent to it, a group of four,
Three women and a man who held
A wire arch like a witching wand.
Where, ladies? he was saying.
Then they came to the outside ramp.
A new addition, just wide enough
For a gurney, the manager said.
They filed up and could touch
The blistered paint on the wall.
We won't need to sandblast now, said the manager.
Inside, it was sunnier than below.
All the doors were open and most
Lying in bed had curtains open.
The committee, glancing in, saw
The sick smiling back or asleep.
The nurse, a crisp New Zealander,
Opened the windows, she said, twice a day,
Sun or snow, rain or wind.
The committee nodded, but each
Worried too late to ask.
The manager said, Mother is here.
In one room where curtains were drawn
Lay a figure with a sheet laid on lightly,
Salmon-rouged cheeks,
Bluish curls cropped close.
Mother, the manager whispered, won't you be glad
To leave here? She snored a little.
Mother's asleep, he said. But she will be glad.

They left the nest of invalids,
Hearing, below, a glissando of bells.
The dinner call, the manager explained.
In the hall of the east wing
There was John with a glockenspiel

Hammering and slurring the steel keys,
An unlit cigar—the same?—
Plugged in the side of his mouth.
Doors opened, and women in print dresses,
Stooped as if to peer around corners,
Walked out, keeping that posture.
There were a few couples, too,
Men smaller than their women.
Though the single men, like John,
Seemed stronger, dapper, knotting ties
And setting their faces toward dinner.
The manager guided the committee
Among the slow moving line,
Here and there falling in step
With an old woman or man.
Aren't these floors cold and hard, Mary?
And to the croquet players,
We'll have a big game room at the new place.
The faces aimed ahead, bemused,
As if voices pestered them
After they'd switched off their hearing aids.
The manager led the committee to the kitchen.
I want you to see this, he said.
A yellow cavern, though clean
(All was clean everywhere
Except where edges crumbled
And no sponging could check the decay).
Two huge female cooks and two
Whip-thin serving women worked up
A batch of chipped beef for dinner.
All this will change, of course.
Seated among the twenty or so tables,
The manager pointed to pictures on walls,
Mostly oblongs of oily twilight,
Sepias, faded earth tones.
These will go, too, the manager said.
We want friendly, vivid colors.

And when one of the committee,
A woman the manager's age or older,
Asked why all were so silent, "sullen," she said,
The manager stopped chewing and listened.
China and silver clicked and clacked
Mocking the clip-clop of false teeth.
And he sighed, but first joked
That everyone must be hungry.
They are looking at us, she said, "glaring."
And the other committee members,
One older, one younger man, nodded.
They are waiting to learn who you are, of course.
So the manager rose, his napkin sliding
Off his lap to the floor, and spoke.
Good evening, everyone. He was answered
By a grumble of full mouths.
I am showing our guests the new site after supper,
Where already our new home is underway.
Better hurry, someone said.
Bye-bye, said another.
The manager did not sit down but smiled, Shall we go?

They drove along silently,
Each thinking, and the manager feeling
His heart cramped and pressed for time
Since it was growing dark and he needed
Light to show off the building.

Nothing these three might do could stop it.
The foundations were laid, the skeleton up,
The wiring being installed and all
Would be better than what they had seen.
Surely they knew this. He drove.
He would almost have spoken his mind
As the streetlights began to glow softly.
Instead, he sped up, rounding the hill
Where the new home looked out at the city
And the vast green of a cemetery,
Which he was persuaded resembled a golf course

And offered the peace of a golf course.
They found as they rounded the bend
They were the first on the scene
Of the fire that lit up the building site
Like a cage of glowworms. Just beginning,
It burst into glory as the car stopped.

No, it was only the sunset, turning
The bare studs and struts to charcoal.
If they would follow him, said the manager,
He would show them the evening vista
Over the rolling lawns below,
The flat slabs of polished granite
Like windows of coral light. Do you see?
He asked the committee. Look at it.
They looked. They saw everything.

The Death of God

A man whose wife's enlarged heart was going learned of a
    drug
That would enlarge the mind. The couple was old, but
    enlarging
The mind with a drug was a new idea. Make the date late
    Eisenhower, early Kennedy.
The couple was old, not born in this century, and the
    woman's heart,
Stretched in girlhood by rheumatic fever, spread like an
    open hand
Between her lungs on the X ray. The doctor made a fist
    against
The wide shadow of it to show her husband a healthy heart
    size.
Soon she was floating near death, like a balloon trailing a
    string
Along the surface of lawns and swimming pools, waiting to
    snag
Or sink at last among low shrubs or roses, and he grew
    impatient.
Now this man pastored a church he had founded based on
    his belief
That the supernatural power of creation was ours for a
    prayer.
He sold vitamins, royal jelly, *The Autobiography of a Yogi*
    in the lobby.
He preached about his dreams and spoke of archetypes.
He discovered people, like the man who knew Methuselah,
    the girl from the Pleiades.
He had many followers. The church was in Greater Los
    Angeles.
But his wife and he had entered old age unhappy with each
    other,
She, with his character flaws; he, with her physical
    weakness.
She scorned the people he drew around him, their unhealthy
Vegetarian complexions, their talk of auras. He resented the
    slowness
Of every action she executed just to endure a single day,

And hired a live-in nurse, to free him. Then, he discovered
   the drug.
A doctor placed the first dose on his tongue, and he had
   confirmed
His belief that the body is a radiant intersection of
   enormous power,
Even his aging and shrinking body that had been apart from
   hers so long.
He would cure her with its touch. But she drifted just at
   the lip of death,
Like a child trailing her fingers along the top of a garden
   wall,
Turning the tips black with dead lichen and dust, and he
   turned away.
He went for another dose and became convinced
That the ornate richness of his life and thought and
   friendships
Was an edifice like Chartres, and clearly, like the Pyramids,
Gave proof of otherworldly powers converging in him.
If only he could show her the glorious niche where, carved
   in granite,
She took her place with saints. But he found her hovering,
Like a soap bubble that a breath repels, a finger can shatter.
He watched death crawl on her like iridescence, like
   vitreous floaters on air.
She had led him from childhood, holding his hand to her
   breast,
Holding his hand when they slept in single beds, holding
   him
At arm's length so she could catch her breath. How small
   the world was
And now how large. The little god he had worshipped hung
   on a pin
In the doll's house of the past. That was why her heart
   failed.
It, too, had outgrown the world. He understood. The nurse
   took his elbow
And whispered. The bed where his wife lay seemed part of
   a larger world,

Its four posts topped with flames, the chenille bedspread a
       white plain,
And his only access to her the winding route of the
       breathing tube,
Connecting the heavy medieval dome of the oxygen tank
And, at the nostrils, the frail mask of the face.
He would travel it. The nurse tugged, whispered. He
       stopped the car.
The white desert beyond the mountains was whiter in the
       moonlight,
And simple, only the moonlit tabletop and the moon.
For this he hardly needed the drug. The highway crossed
       from the bulbous
Moon's face into the faint promise, like an aura, along the
       horizon.
He would travel it. Death was larger than the body, like the
       mind
Radiating from him on the tips of his senses and meeting
       the crowd of stars.
How powerful the stars were, yet he had seen them fall.
He had watched them rain, when the century turned, when
       the god
He had worshipped was a child like him and became a
       woman
Who held him and led him along a route he was glad to
       take,
Into the enlarging heart of the world, where prayer was
       answered
By a touch, a glad cry, and a deep sleep. She woke, gasped,
And had no final words and needed the nurse's mouth on
       hers,
Crossed hands on her breastbone pumping. They needed
       his voice—
Not the voice of infinite space—to call for help at the speed
       of light
From the small house in Greater Los Angeles, where God
       was going quickly.

Sea-Fig

for Donald Justice

In my new country we will keep this plant.
Let them accuse me of nostalgia. That is,
If I allow critics in the first place.
I want sea-fig and ice plant on the cliffs,
And cliffs, of course, sheer but not mountainous,
Rimming the beaches of secluded coves.
By God, I want these fleshy purple flowers,
Bearding the cliffs, draping, festooning them!
That's all I want. Everything else I want
To startle me. No, there should be the ocean
As I recall it, changing colors, contained.
Pelicans, too, cruising a moon-shaped bay,
In tandem, turning sideways on crooked wings
To fall right at a fish. You should see them—
And will as soon as you arrive; then, faintly,
The yellow and magenta tendriled eyes
Of ice plant and my sea-fig—succulents!
And mountains in the background (I will live
Above the water, over my own dock,
And fall asleep at night to lapping wavelets
And hear the swells roll in and try to break),
A range to match the crescent of the bay,
Perpetually green with redwood, laurel,
(I see you know my model) and madrone.
From up there we will get word of bad things,
Wilderness atrocities. This will come
Unofficially on the lips of vagrants—
Always alone but gathering downtown
(I want a town) with backpacks, sacks, and bags,
Sunburned or pale, all hungry more or less,
And implicated by their frazzled lies
Or simply meditating, beyond facts,
Because they know and we don't want to. Well,
We may want to, and so they must be there.
One in particular, a window washer
Who sets his bucket down outside a store
And does one window free, then goes inside
Where they have watched and almost always say
No, they don't need their windows washed. He stows

His sleeping bag beneath a drooping cedar
In a waste ground beside the haunted lighthouse.
I'll find him, mop and bucket on his shoulder,
Setting out after breakfast, and I'll hire him.
It will be a mistake, a tragic one,
For one of us.
                        I'll start to listen to him,
Once he has put his washing gear away
And joined me on a sail to check the view
Of my new country. Thus at liberty
To speak, resting with tiller underarm,
He will begin with things I never knew.
Pointing at an outcrop on a peak
Or at a firebreak down a mountainside
Or, closer, at the opaque hazy square
Of window in a gable among rooftops,
He'll spin a line out from his fingertip
And I will follow, listening to his story.
A face will hover everywhere he points.
Its features, always sadly skewed by pain,
I know I wouldn't want to see for real.
But now, because they're printed like a smudge
On each new landmark, I will have to see—
To see and know. At last, when we come up
Beside the pier, he'll hush me, though I'm silent.
And I will hear the seals I thought we left
On their rookery opposite the lighthouse,
Croaking, groaning, at the far end of the bay.
They swim between the two spots, back and forth,
All day, all night—I hear him telling me.
They flop up on the crossbeams of the pier.
Lying along the narrow boards, the cows
Suckle their calves. The bulls insist on climbing
Over them, fluttering like butterflies.
How does he know all this? A piping shrillness,
Which hits my eardrum every time he tells me
Something I didn't know, will turn to envy.
And he will start to look uncomfortable
And tell me less.

Try to arrive by day.
It's best to swing wide, outside the seal rock,
And cut across the bay, behind the breakers.
This way you'll see the cliffs taper from right
To left down to the pier, and underneath
The greatest mass of purple sea-fig, my place—
Halfway along the arc, exactly where
You're aimed. But if you come by night, drop anchor
Beyond the seal rock, wait there until morning.
There is a lighthouse, as I've said before,
A haunted one. Don't trust the light it throws.
But in the sunshine, when the fog's burned off,
We'll take a closer look at everything.
Especially the sea-fig, which must be,
I am convinced, the body's analogue.
Its leaves are pulpy, and, if you can skin
The epidermis off, the membrane shines
Painfully, and the outer sheath of green,
Clinging to your fingers, appears transparent.
But even more revealing is the flower—
That is the real iris of the eye.
The blossom of the sea-fig or the ice plant,
The eye's plant, looks like filaments of color
Around the pupil. Flowers of the flesh,
Hung on the cliffs to watch and to be watched.
Don't let me see reproach, don't let me see it,
In your eyes. Let me be the only one
Who knows and tells you.

Testimony and Postscript

Once I was someone coming out of the dark
Out of somebody's past to greet him again,
And once I have myself been greeted like that,
Out of the dark, my past, by someone I, too,
Had forgotten. All this is quite literal.
I stood in my college quad watching a dance
One night, this was in California, the music
Had begun suddenly in a dormitory window
And grown, as the sun went down behind hills,
Louder as the dim quad lights, hidden in ivy,
Lit paths into the surrounding buildings.
We were silhouettes, many danced by themselves,
And I was looking for a girl I hardly knew
And spotted her, dancing alone, her arms scissoring
The private space I was too timid to claim.
I watched her, the leotard-smooth shadow of her,
And from a bunch of shadows nearby a voice
Came saying my name and then he stood there.
His beard, black as a watchband, and that hairline
That joined his eyebrows in a single cloud,
Made me remember him, and his voice,
As timid as my distance from that girl.
I can't tell you how long ago I had known him.
He had sailed to Mexico, and above Acapulco,
The ship or boat—I couldn't quite picture it—
Had broken up in a storm, along a shore
At dawn, so that the sun rising behind it
Made a serrated line of peaks look volcanic.
He swam in shallow water for his life,
So sick with adrenaline when he washed up
He vomited for sheer joy repeatedly.
His voice, trembling, afraid of its own shadow,
Told me all this in a few strange seconds.
He said that he would sell his story, he hoped,
To *National Geographic* or *Reader's Digest.*
The girl I wanted to fall in love with
Had disappeared completely while he spoke.
And as if he knew he had only half my attention
He was gone, too, saying, "See you around."

And I had said that, once, one night at the door
Of a girl I wanted to surprise in Pasadena.
"See you around," I had said, after she hugged me
Mechanically, puzzled that, on a rainy night,
After her boyfriend had charged away on his Honda,
This forgotten person she had met at youth camp
Should appear at her door. He must have been nearby,
Watching her kiss her boyfriend good night.
How strange it was. He told her his future,
Where it was taking him, and asked her hers,
Which she admitted was going to be here,
In Pasadena. Then, "See you around,"
He had said and got in a van parked up the street,
Full of people, his friends perhaps, and drove
Out of her life, her half of a memory
He would never know the worth of, if it had one.

But this is not enough to convince you.
I have met the man I saw once in the bus depot
In San Francisco. He walked back and forth,
Looming and in clown-sized, worn-out shoes,
Under the cruddy light as most of us waited.
A man in a neat suit tried to talk to him.
He tried to remind him that they knew each other.
But when the walker understood, he broke
His pattern and walked out into the street,
The sane little questioner calling after him.
I knew I would never forget their faces,
Especially the madman's like a gray lamp,
Pointed down at the one he wouldn't talk to.
I recognized him again years later, elsewhere,
It doesn't matter. What does is that he
Remembered that year and how he walked
And walked until he remembered his life,
Broke down, and looked for home. He wasn't sure,
But he thought the other man had been his brother.

Miss Urquhart's Tiara

For Chase Twichell

I know this can't mean anything at all,
Except I found the fringed phacelia
Today, walking with my daughters beyond
The baseball diamond, and remembered reading
A story called "Miss Urquhart's Tiara"
So long ago, remembering it surprised me,
Like the Smoky Mountain flower shading white
To the pale blue of skies this time of year,
All the way from the mountains four hours east.
From one flower clouds amassed.
The story built its paragraphs.
And the grass, thick as the stumbling talk
That goes on in my head, tripped me here and there
As when I'm alone I fall into speech
(The habit worries me, when I can see myself
An old man snarled in monologues).
The fringed phacelia. Miss Urquhart.
Strange, their names meant nothing to each other.

Or to my daughters. The toddler doubled
Over a tuft of grass she hugged for balance.
Her older sister drifted at the edge
Of calling range, the fringe of cottonwoods
Along the stream that cuts our neighborhood
And draws the network nobody thinks of
Except in flood, except the city planner
Who, I imagine, knows the map by heart
Like his palm's creasework. All it is is drainage,
Though clear weather clears the water,
And clams, crayfish, snails with turbinate shells
Come to life. There's a faint tinge of odor,
And up the bank, a humped concrete manhole
Reads "Sanitary Sewer." We don't care.
I showed the little one the blue-white flower.
She took it, put it in her mouth, and ate it.
Her sister called. The poplar she stood under
Was the spine of a green book I reached for.

The story of "Miss Urquhart's Tiara,"
Which I hold open in my lap somewhere
On a peninsula, in a hotel,
In a fall noted there for peaks of color
Washed out by rain, was written by someone
You often find in such anthologies,
Reserved for rain in hotels on peninsulas,
Stevenson or Saki, Maugham or Kipling.
In it, two children, brother and sister,
Take a walk one spring day with their teacher
(It may be Scotland, it may be Stevenson).
It's a long walk, but the children keep up
For the first mile. The road's border of nettles
Prickles the boy's bare legs. His sister pales.
A heavy dew crowns weeds and spiderwebs,
And there's a taste of steam in the air.
The sky looks like a pane of whitewashed glass.

Wide shouldered and wide eyed, their smiling friend,
Miss Urquhart, urges them, reaching a hand
To each. Soon they will leave their native land
For—India? (Kipling?)—for a distant country,
And she wants them to have a memory
Of such a day as this that will filter back
Through another climate's heat waves and dust.
But when the children learn it's two miles yet,
They add a whine to the field's insect drone.
Thirsty—they're thirsty. She finds them stalks
Of timothy to chew. They're both too big
To be carried and yet still young enough
To want to be, saying their daddy would.
On they plod, and Miss Urquhart slowly sees
This outing as a bad job, proposed for
The parents' sake, grateful, interesting people
Wound up in packing twine, and for the children,
Wilting and peevish now, but who adore her.

The girl plops down, defeated, in her jumper.
The boy scratches his legs. Miss Urquhart pulls him

Dockweed leaves to rub them, then tells why
They have to keep walking and not turn back.
Ahead there is a church—oh, they don't care!
Once, I was to be married there, she says.
Now, this is a secret, you can't tell.
But if you'll walk with me, you'll hear it.
Are you married, Miss Urquhart? they both ask.
No, and that doesn't matter one bit now.
I want to see this church again. But if
I tell you why, you have to listen and keep up.
No more bubbling babies. Now, take my hands.
There's a town, too, where we can have our tea.
And she tows the children through it all,
The landscape, the fatigue, the tale she tells.
Hedges back away to give them room,
The dew dries, nettles reach but do not touch.

She was engaged, a long, long time ago,
To the headmaster of the little school
There, where they are going. She was his first.
Whereas, she'd had boyfriends. How many boyfriends?
Boys at church, at school, at dances, boys
To walk with on this very road to town,
Which there, you see, is cropping up just now,
And there's the church, that tuft of sooty stone.
And that's the church where you were to be married?
Yes, and I even know the pastor still.
He'll give us tea. And why were you not married?
You know, she says, not everybody must be.
You can be very happy all alone.
And are you very happy, Miss Urquhart?
I am, very. And why were you not married?
He went away, to Australia. I stayed.
They step into the small, cool church, and meet
The pastor, who gives them tea and takes them home.

He went away because he was not loved.
He gave her a tiara, to wear on their honeymoon
In the capital—Edinburgh or London.

The little crown had been a great-aunt's bequest
To him for his bride. He gave it to her
Too soon, it seems, because he asked for it back.
Then gave it again, set it on her head.
Then asked for it back, left for Australia.
You can be very happy all alone.
But this part, winding through her on the ride back,
Never reaches the children's ears. She catches
Her breath, repeating, "Gave. Then, took. Gave."
Had she said it aloud? No one had noticed.
She leaves the children touchingly, says farewell
To the grateful, interesting parents,
And turns back into the hidden channels
Of her story. Not is she happy, but how
Did he, who loved her, make himself happier?

The last time they sat up late in her room,
The window held the summer's hour of darkness,
And they were silent, watching through this night
That would end soon, an easy vigil, when,
Speaking to someone else (a dream companion?),
He said, Yes, he had dreamed of Australia
All of his life, the Outback painted
With runes that someday he would read.
Someday. She knew she didn't love him
Enough to tease him for this, but instead
Thought of the tiara in its hinged box,
The almost satiny pearls, the almost cold
Diamonds, the almost tarnished web of silver
They studded, and the ritual of giving,
Then taking it back to have a stone reset,
A broken silver filament resoldered.
Whatever it was worth, it was enough,
She knew it now, to get to Australia.

She turns away, having told the children
Only enough to keep them satisfied
And us only enough to keep us reading.
The front door closes as she turns away,

The street lamps are lit up, Australia
Is a lost continent. But do you know,
Miss Urquhart, that I remember the cool leaf
Of dockweed rubbing up and down my calf,
And how you trailed us, my sister and me,
Behind you like a wake, how we kept up,
Questioning you just as you'd intended,
And getting for all our curiosity
A cup of tea? Today, among clouds
Of fringed phacelia in the deep grass,
When my daughters heard me speak to someone
They couldn't see, they waited for an answer.
So did I, even though I held their hands.
It took them pressing close to close the book.

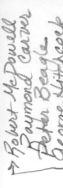

About the Author

The many places in which Mark Jarman has lived have become
settings for his poetry—from Santa Maria and Redondo Beach, California,
to Kirkcaldy, Scotland, where his minister father served parishes, to the
American Midwest and Italy, where he has studied and worked.
Jarman is now associate professor of English at Vanderbilt University
in Nashville; in 1989–90 he will be in England, directing Vanderbilt's
program at the University of Leeds. A graduate of the University of
California, Santa Cruz (B.A. 1974) and the University of Iowa (M.F.A.
1976), he is the author of three other books of poetry, *North Sea, The
Rote Walker,* and *Far and Away.* Jarman is also coeditor of the literary
journal *The Reaper.* He has received a Joseph Henry Jackson award, an
Academy of American Poets prize, and two NEA grants, in 1977 and in
1983, the last in support of the poems written for this book. His home is
in Nashville.

About the Book

The Black Riviera is composed in ITC Garamond. Garamond, named
for the sixteenth-century French type designer Claude Garamond, was
introduced in the United States by American Type Foundry in 1919,
when their cutting, based on the *caractères de l'Université* of the
Imprimerie Nationale, appeared. Many other versions were made for
Linotype, Monotype, Intertype, Ludlow, and the Stempel foundry. The
face has since been adapted for phototypesetting, CRT typesetting, and
laser typesetting. The book was composed by WorldComp of Sterling,
Virginia, and designed by Kachergis Book Design of Pittsboro, North
Carolina.

Wesleyan University Press, 1990